Together Forever!

"One of the most simple, practical, 'must-read' books on relationships that I've ever read. . . . What is most important is that the authors walk their talk."
—Gerald G. Jampolsky, M.D., and Diane V. Cirincione, authors of *Change Your Mind, Change Your Life*

⁓

"Presenting words of wisdom in a simple and clear style is a difficult task—the Richfields have accomplished this beautifully in their lovely and loving book."
—Susanna McMahon, Ph.D., author of *The Portable Therapist*

⁓

"It brings a new dimension to a loving marriage."
—Pat and Chris Riley
Pat Riley is the coach of the Miami Heat and author of *The Winner Within*

⁓

"[The Richfields] celebrate our society's return to old-fashioned values and show readers how they can experience the deep satisfaction and happiness that a fully alive marriage can bring."
—*Westlaker Times* (Lorain, Ohio)

⁓

"PRACTICAL GUIDELINES FOR A HEALTHY, SATISFYING MARRIAGE."
—*DeForest Times-Tribune* (Wisc.)

TOGETHER FOREVER!

125 LOVING WAYS TO HAVE A VITAL AND ROMANTIC MARRIAGE

❧

LEW RICHFIELD, PH.D.
AND
GLORIA RICHFIELD, PH.D.

A DELL TRADE PAPERBACK

A DELL TRADE PAPERBACK

Published by
Dell Publishing
a division of
Bantam Doubleday Dell Publishing Group, Inc.
1540 Broadway
New York, New York 10036

ISBN: 0-440-50780-4

Reprinted by arrangement with Delacorte Press

Printed in the United States of America

Published simultaneously in Canada

January 1997

10 9 8 7 6 5 4 3 2 1

BVG

CONTENTS

For
Blythe Jane,
Tom,
Pamela,
Julia,
and Owen

ACKNOWLEDGMENTS

There are many couples who played prominent roles in the formation of the concepts we have presented in this book. We are deeply indebted to all those who have shared their ideas and experiences with us. Some presented the problems we address in the book, some were role models, and others we had long conversations with about relationships.

It has been our good fortune to have many dynamic people in our lives who have been instrumental in influencing our paths. We are grateful to Marcia Seligson, author and friend, for her special support.

We want to thank Trish Todd of Delacorte Press for her belief in us, and her enthusiasm for our work.

We also wish to express our appreciation to Lorie Cox of West Coast Word Processing for her outstanding word processing skills, as well as her patience, cooperation, and availability during the stressful moments.

Our special thanks go to Jody Rein, our extraordinary agent and guide, who gave so much of her time and energy to this manuscript and who has become a cherished friend.

Unusual as it may seem, we want to acknowledge each other for meeting the latest delightful challenge in our marriage—the incredible task of blending our words to express our thoughts in *Together Forever!* We were obliged to confront our differences during the writing of every page and completed the manuscript with renewed mutual respect. We are very excited about the discovery of yet one more way to collaborate.

INTRODUCTION

After we were married in 1949 and began living together for the first time, the only model of a happily married couple we had was Ozzie and Harriet. They seemed to have the perfect family. Our own union featured Lew, carrying around memories of World War II and trying to figure out what to do with his life, and Gloria, soon up to her knees in children and housekeeping, wondering where all the romance had gone. What a shock it was to discover that real life was more like our parents' marriages, which in retrospect we realize were filled with despair and resignation. So without any realistic model for our marriage, we muddled through.

As we look back on our forty-six years together, we can see three distinct marriages within one. During the first ten years, we were totally unconscious. We kept bumping into each other, completely confused. We had two children, changed jobs and moved five times. We kept so busy we didn't have time to think about our marriage. However we both knew something was missing. During our "second marriage" we awakened to our discontent. We tried, but couldn't figure out how to communicate with one another in ways that we both understood. There was a lot of blaming and accusing. We didn't have a clue about how to get to the real issues that divided us. No matter how hard we tried, we continued to unconsciously sabotage our efforts to work it out. We had met the enemy and it was us.

This put us on the road to our "third marriage." We found a therapist who taught us how to communicate with one another. We learned how to take the chance of being completely open, expressing ourselves on a more intimate level, and trusting each other's ability to handle our vulnerability with care. The growing richness in our marriage allowed us to focus on other issues that required serious attention. In our early fifties, we were learning that we could have it all. We decided to change our lifestyle in order to achieve our new goal, which was to become psychotherapists. We decided to enroll in college as freshmen. Together we attained our bachelor degrees, then ultimately our doctorates and licenses as marriage and family therapists. The excitement of achieving these goals in mid-life brought us even closer together.

Our experiences of living and working together through the difficulties that life presents to us all, coupled with our training and our experience working with many

INTRODUCTION

troubled couples in our private practice, have brought us to the creation and the writing of Together Forever!

It is our fervent hope that as you read Together Forever! you will learn more about yourself and your partner. You will become more fully alive and engaged in one another's life.

We believe marriage is a shared vision and an ongoing process of change. No one really "gets there." There is always opportunity for deeper and deeper intimacy. We believe the basic keys to a lasting, alive, and satisfying marriage are: Love, Equality, Partnership, Passion, Communication, Commitment—AND THE DETERMINATION TO KEEP THE MARRIAGE A HIGH PRIORITY IN LIFE.

We have divided Together Forever! into seven chapters that correspond to the main issues that create confusion in a marriage. Each entry describes a situation that occurs in most marriages. We may have left some out. We hope you will let us know what they are, so we can include them in future volumes of Together Forever!

We offer this book to you in your loving journey together.

Gloria and Lew

It has always been important to us to acknowledge that abilities and behaviors can apply to either gender at any given time. Therefore, throughout this book, substitute "her" for "him" and "him" for "her" wherever appropriate.

PARTNERING

LEW

When I was fifty-five years old, I was invited to go on a trip to learn technical rock climbing. Though we were to be well instructed, there would certainly be an element of danger in our adventure.

When I told Gloria how badly I wanted to go, she initially said nothing. We both know that when you're on the side of a granite wall, accidents can happen that are not like stumbling over a crack in the sidewalk or bumping your head against the roof of your car. I conveniently ignored the fact of my age and continued to think of myself as I was when I was younger and more physically adept, and Gloria was kind enough not to bring my age to my attention.

I could see her compose herself silently, weighing real fears for my safety against her desire to encourage me in my dreams. She drew a line, made her decision, and spoke. I don't remember her words. I do remember the unconditional backing as she put her fears aside and expressed excitement that matched my own about the trip.

I left home with her words of encouragement in my ears. I truly believe I was safer on my adventure because of her support. I had the confidence and ability to concentrate that I

PARTNERING

may not have mustered if I had believed Gloria was not behind me in this new endeavor.

The experience of testing myself turned out to be more validating and exciting than I could have hoped. I discovered a deeper knowledge of myself in relationship to Gloria and an ever-increasing appreciation of the support she offered me.

RICHFIELDS'
Rule 1

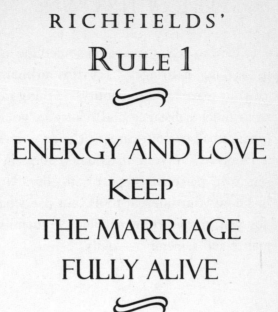

ENERGY AND LOVE
KEEP
THE MARRIAGE
FULLY ALIVE

GIVE YOUR MARRIAGE
A LIFE OF ITS OWN

It's very hard to keep focused on something as nebulous as "my marriage." Try this mental shift. Think of your marriage as an entity—a thing in your life with as much substance and reality as your passion for basketball or your career or even your house or your family. Give your marriage a form in your mind—its own personal shape or identity. No one needs to know your internal tools, but use whatever works for you to give your marriage an identity you can visualize and remember—daily.

LAY THE FOUNDATION OF TRUST FROM THE BEGINNING

Trust is the first building block in the construction of a successful marriage. Because of its power and strength, it is important to nurture trust through continuing honesty. If the relationship is a priority, then trust must be, too. Remember:

- Keep his secrets private.
- Honor his need for confidentiality on certain subjects.
- Do what you say you're going to do.
- Do the things that are important to him.

DEMONSTRATE YOUR RESPECT FOR YOUR PARTNER—PUBLICLY AND PRIVATELY

Familiarity in a marriage seems to breed not contempt, but integration. Day after day it gets easier to forget your partner is a separate being deserving of your respectful treatment. Tie these tips around your finger to remember:

- Think often of your engagement and the fact that you made with it a choice—at the time the biggest choice of your life. Treat your partner with the honor such a weighty choice deserves.

- Listen to your mate with the attentiveness you would show a friend. Publicly demonstrate your respect for him by listening to his stories, avoiding denigration, and withholding your critical judgment.

- Stick this reminder in your wallet: *Intimacy is not a license to toss aside basic social kindness.*

MAKE YOUR MARRIAGE AS IMPORTANT AS THE WEDDING

For many couples, wedding planning and the wedding day itself become almost an obsession. Nothing else is on their minds for months. The wedding happens. It's wonderful, or traumatic, or somewhere in between. Then it's over—and attention returns to your previous priorities—jobs, finances, hobbies. It's easy to forget you have a new priority in your lives—your marriage.

Don't forget it! Try these tools:

• Make "pay attention to" as important a vow as "loving," "honoring," or whatever you vowed to each other.

• When life's other demands take up much of your time, give your partner the assurance that the relationship remains the most important part of your life.

SEE DOUBLE

Think of your marriage as a double rainbow: Each color is a thing of incredible beauty; two together are a single miracle.

COOK TOGETHER

Even the most democratic of couples, those who take turns cooking and cleaning in the kitchen, may be missing out on one of the most enjoyable activities you can do together, particularly when it seems you have no time for each other. Make meal planning and cooking a joint effort. Take turns being head chef and running the show. Don't be above chopping, slicing, or washing veggies—you'll find it's a great time to practice your teamwork, chat about your day, dance, joke—just to be together, productively.

DISCOVER THE JOY OF BEING IN A PARTNERSHIP

Whatever happens to one of you happens to both of you. If you share your individual experiences, both good and bad, you will be a team, cooperating openly, gaining strength. If you don't talk about your individual experiences, they will still affect the relationship. Underground and unspoken, they will create distance between you. Count on it.

Being partners has less to do with who does the dishes or walks the dog than it has to do with openly sharing and taking interest in the details of each other's life. When you fully participate in each other's life, you'll find your marriage blooms into a life of its own.

RICHFIELDS'
Rule 2
❧

MARRIAGE
IS A
LICENSE
TO
LOVE

❧

RELISH THE YIN AND THE YANG

If your partner is good at finances and you're not, shout hallelujah! If your partner is quicker at word games, play anyway. Marriage is not a competitive game. Enjoy those special skills your partner brings. In the partnership of marriage, they add to your skills. Sit back and let your partner do what she does better. Don't feel inadequate—try feeling proud!

IF IT'S IMPORTANT TO YOUR PARTNER, AND RELATIVELY INCONSEQUENTIAL TO YOU, DO IT

Put the toilet seat down. Don't blow your nose at the dinner table. Snap the lid on the contact lens solution. The only reason to hold on to habits that irritate your partner, and don't mean anything to you, is to maintain power or control, and that's not a good reason. Give in and give it up.

DON'T EXPECT HIM TO BE
WHO HE'S NOT

When your partner fails to fulfill your expectations of how he should look and behave, take a close look at yourself before you take a critical swipe at him. Do you expect him to be just like you? Maybe the orange shirt and pink slacks *are* appropriate on the golf course, as much as they turn your stomach. Let him be who he is.

FIND TIME TO GET
AWAY—TOGETHER

Make a date with your mate, but don't always go to dinner and a movie. Every now and then, especially if you find you're always surrounded by people or connected to your cellular phone, schedule time together separate from the rest of your life. Take a walk in the park. Go for a drive. Have a picnic. Restore each other's psyche. You need to get to know each other, and recognize each other, over and over again.

RESPECT YOUR PARTNER'S NEED FOR PRIVACY

When your partner is lost in thought, asking "What are you thinking?" may make him feel that you're staging an invasion. While sharing thoughts is valuable to the relationship and deepens intimacy, it has to be natural and voluntary—everyone has the right to the privacy of his own thoughts.

It's fine to ask, "Would you like to talk about what you're thinking?" Just remember, if he says "No," or "Not right now," he's not rejecting you. Give him time to just be.

ENTERTAIN IN YOUR HOME
AS A TEAM

Don't forget you are both hosts to whomever visits your home, even if the visitor is closer to your partner than to you. You are now part of a team, there's no valid argument in "He's your friend, you deal with him." Take an active role in doing whatever tasks are involved in making your guest comfortable. The experience of entertaining will be much easier on you both that way, and the effort you make will pay for itself in the closeness you'll feel, the appreciation you'll receive—and the help you'll get when your friend (or mother) next comes to visit.

RELY ON THE POWER OF TWO ...

When you're overwhelmed by one of life's curve balls, your natural reaction may be to go silent, close down, assume no one wants to hear the long story of your woes. Instead, repeat this mantra: "He wants to hear. He wants to know. He wants to help." Then, talk.

In so doing, you build up the foundation of an intimate relationship, rather than more walls between you.

... AND EMPOWER THE TWO!

Your partner is exhibiting her usual signs of being preoccupied or anxious. She's at the refrigerator, or biting her fingernails, or spacing out, or whatever you know are signs of trouble. You want to help, but you don't know how to break through, and the last thing you want to do is intrude. We often feel powerless and alone in the face of our partner's troubles.

You can help—but not by asking "What's wrong?" or "Is something bothering you?" Nine times out of ten such a question will get answered by a sullen "Nothing" or "No." Instead, form your concerns as a statement. State "I want to help," then ask "What can I do for you?" Or, try "I sense something is on your mind. Let's talk about it." You'll both get comfort from restating the theme of your partnership—that you are in this together, no matter what.

DON'T DECIDE WITHOUT HER

Many of us become quite accustomed to making decisions on our own while we're single. For some, the concept of sharing decision making can be quite novel—and difficult. From choosing to buy skim milk versus 2 percent milk, to choosing where to live, all decisions involving the two of you must be joint. If you have trouble discussing your decisions, remember: There's little that makes your partner feel she's less important to you than the feeling that her opinion doesn't count. Ask: "What do you think?" or "Is that okay with you?" Listen to the answer. Your marriage will grow stronger each time you do—and your partner will feel wonderful.

RICHFIELDS'
Rule 3

TRUE LOVE
IS
BUILT ON
EQUALITY

DON'T KEEP SCORE ON HOUSEHOLD CHORES

Guess what? There's no such thing as equality when it comes to household chores. We're not talking about gender—we firmly believe household chores have no gender. But maintaining a perfect balance of equal participation is a futile goal. Each day, each week, someone's going to feel he's pulling more than his share of the load—if you try to divide the load equally. Give it up. Forget about coming up with a fair and equal division of tasks—you'll end up with a dirty house and resentment. Adopt this point of view instead:

• Your mutual goal is that the chores get done so you can have time to have fun together. (Your goal is *not* that each of you gets his own chores done.)

• You divide the tasks by who does what best, and who minds doing what least.

• If one of you doesn't get to a chore—the other pitches in. No tallies allowed.

MONEY ... MONEY ... MONEY

Money can make you sad or make you glad. It all depends on how you think about it. Each of you has brought your own money attitudes, dreams, and goals into your marriage. One thing remains constant, though, in an equal and loving partnership. Regardless of who earns the money, the decisions for how to handle money must be made together in order for trust to be established and the welfare of the couple to be assured.

These are our rules for a compatible money-handling relationship:

• There must be no secrets between you about how money is saved, spent, and/or invested.

• The person who is best at a particular task of money handling, whether it be bookkeeping or investing, should be assigned that task.

• Each partner must have an equal share in the decisions regarding the allocation of money.

• Each partner must have a comfortable amount of WAM (Walkin' Around Money).

• Have conversations about your money as often as necessary to eliminate undue stress.

ESTABLISHING GOALS IS AS IMPORTANT AS FLOSSING EVERY DAY

Set short- and long-term goals in your marriage. It's a fact: Couples who set goals together stay together. Work together to make your dreams happen. A short-term goal could be to get dinner on the table on time for a week. A long-term goal could be as blue sky as building a house in the woods or working on inner growth. Write your goals down and put the list on the refrigerator. Keep the list short.

If you don't achieve your goal, so what? Let it go. Goals are targets, not obligations. Goals can change.

Schedule a goal check-in date—once a month, once every two months, once a year, whatever suits both of you.

(Your first goal: Set a time to talk about goals. Put that date on the calendar today.)

YOU NEVER KNOW WHAT
THEY'RE LIKE AT HOME

It's so easy to fall into the trap of looking at other couples and assuming they're happier, richer, better adjusted, more organized, more together, more anything than you are. Here's the news: They may be, and they may not be. It doesn't matter. Your marriage is your own, different from anyone else's. The longer you're together, the more individual your marriage becomes. Better in some respects, not so good in other respects perhaps—your marriage is all that matters. Let the others go.

A HUG IN THE MORNING CAN JUMP START YOUR DAY

Morning conversation can be a reminder of how pleasurable last night was, even if all you did was sit and talk quietly or watch TV together. Set the alarm for five minutes earlier. Tell each other your dreams and share those intimate feelings. Talk about your plans for the day and kiss before you part. Every day.

WORK IS WORK IS WORK

Many marriages involve one partner working at an office and another managing the home. Regardless of the many media messages to the contrary, many office workers still perceive their jobs as the harder or more valuable. This entrenched view is not easy to change and can hurt the partner at home, making her feel unimportant and unvalued. You each contribute to the partnership. No one is more or less important than the other.

So, now and then, have a simple conversation that confirms the importance of each other's job well done.

MAKE ROOM FOR LAUGHTER

Cultivate your playfulness and sense of humor. When the business of life begins to make you more serious, it's even more important to find ways to be lighthearted and playful. Don't stop yourself or your partner from acting silly. Sometimes clowning around can create laughter that has the power to heal the wounds that life inflicts. Dance in the kitchen while you're setting the table. Run naked through the house (preferably with the curtains closed). Play a kids' board game (use adult prizes). Go roller-skating at a roller rink. Rent a bicycle built for two. Get the script for *Casablanca* and act it out. Harmonize.

CREATE A MISSION STATEMENT FOR YOUR MARRIAGE

Most business plans include a statement employers and employees alike can refer to at a glance to understand why the company exists and what it hopes to achieve (and how). We think a mission statement is an excellent idea for a marriage. Write one together and frame it. Here's ours:

"This marriage is founded on the principles of equality, passion, compassion, communication, and love. We commit ourselves to keep these principles always uppermost in our minds."

COMMUNICATING

GLORIA

We were married about twelve years. It was two o'clock in the morning and my tossing and turning woke Lew up. When he asked me if I was okay, I said, "I want to talk to you about what happened last night."

He looked at me apprehensively. "What happened last night?"

"You left me alone most of the evening among people I didn't know and you know how I hate to make small talk."

His eyes glazed over and he looked away.

I jumped in. "Now you're tuning me out!"

"No, I'm not," he said. "I'm just thinking about last night and trying to understand."

I was still upset. "If you don't understand, why don't you say so? Just ask me."

"It's two o'clock in the morning! Do we have to talk about this right now?"

"Yes! If not now, when?" We both knew that if we postponed the discussion, we wouldn't sleep (or I wouldn't, anyway).

We agreed to try the conversation over. At an earlier time in our marriage, the middle-of-the-night complaint could

COMMUNICATING

have sparked a defensive blowup. Maybe our exhaustion kept our defenses down, but this time we tried something different. I swallowed my pride and told Lew I realized my surprise attack wasn't fair. I tried to use "I" statements, telling him how I felt without accusing him; Lew did his best to ask me how I felt instead of trying to figure it out on his own, or just defending himself.

It worked. We both fell asleep that night—and woke up the next morning—feeling somehow a little closer, a little more understood.

We learned a lot that night, but not so much about how to behave at parties. Sure, our discussion made clear the fact that Lew was more comfortable in new situations than I was, and we discussed how we could both help me out on those occasions. But as time went on, Lew still sometimes forgot to check in with me at gatherings, and I still sometimes got peeved rather than simply walking up to him and touching base myself. The most important thing we learned was how to feel heard without being attacked or ignored, and that made us feel acknowledged, appreciated, in love, and alive. We like that feeling, so we try to talk in this new way as much as we can!

The funny thing is, although we didn't—couldn't—correct the party problem overnight and prevent all bad feelings in the future, our marriage felt stronger.

TOGETHER FOREVER!

A FEW
MINUTES OF
CONVERSATION
CAN PREVENT
A FEW WEEKS
(OR EVEN YEARS)
OF DISCONTENT

NEVER DELIBERATELY HURT YOUR PARTNER

After you've lived with your partner for a while, you learn just what you can say or do to hurt him: what subtle criticism he's most sensitive to, which old mistake you can throw at him in the heat of an argument, what sarcastic remark you can make in public that will most embarrass him. Don't do it. That's a rule.

P.S. If you find yourself tempted to get those digs in—or you do so and get pleasure from it, it's definitely time to talk—you're keeping something inside that's squealing to get out, showing up in ineffective, destructive ways.

HANDLING THOSE
DELICATE ISSUES

There are times when, for your own peace of mind or your true concern for your partner's well-being, you feel you must (again) bring up a subject that you know is going to be painful for her to hear. Things like her mother, her unhealthy eating, whatever you know she is sensitive about.

First, hold those thoughts until she's ready to hear them.

Second, make a statement. "I'm really uncomfortable about a phone call I just had with your mother and I need to talk with you about it. I need you to help me work this out—I can't do this one alone."

Third, open your heart to her heart. When you share your concerns, speak with care and love and consideration of her feelings, not anger, frustration, or a need to vent.

LEARN THE ART OF DISCUSSION

Very often, a simple discussion can turn into an argument seemingly out of the blue. This happens for concrete reasons that are reparable. Something you said, or the way you said it, pushed your partner's buttons and he reacts defensively, angrily, or simply inappropriately. Stop the argument before it starts. Instead, say "Whoa. Let's take a moment to figure out what's going on right now, and then get back to our discussion. I have a feeling that something I've just said really bothered you, and I'm confused because I didn't intend it to. Can we talk about what just happened?"

LET YOUR PARTNER KNOW
WHEN YOU NEED HER

When you are having a troubling time, let her know so that you get the emotional support you want. If you test your partner's love by waiting to see if she notices your need, you do the marriage a great disservice.

WE NEED TO TALK

No matter how important the subject, nothing turns your partner's blood to ice water faster than the words "We need to talk." Instead of listening, many of us shut down, turn off and disappear. Next time you need to talk, say: "I want to talk about something, and I want you to listen," followed by:

"It's not about you," or

"It's about something that happened to me," or

"It's something we're doing to one another."

By talking this way, you will lower your partner's anxiety and defenses and make way for better understanding.

ASK IF HE WANTS YOUR HELP

Control your desire to solve his problem unless he asks you. Your solving his problem is not necessarily what he wants. Ask, specifically, "How can I help you?" He may want you just to listen—or only to contribute one or two ideas.

COMMUNICATE ON SCHEDULE

Everyone says the key to a happy relationship is communication, but obviously "everyone" doesn't live in the real world, where there is hardly time to do the dishes, much less have a meaningful conversation.

Try this: Schedule a regular fifteen-minute *Check It Out* break once or twice a week, when the two of you are alone. Reconnect. Ask, "How are you doing in your life?" and listen to the answer with attention, love, and support. Take turns.

HONOR YOUR PARTNER'S FEELINGS

Even if her feelings make no sense to you, have regard for them. Recognize you don't experience situations the same way she does. One of the most demeaning things you can do is to dismiss her reality. When she says she's cold—or hurt—or angry, don't jump in with, "Don't be angry," or "You shouldn't be hurt." Instead, listen. Ask for more information if you don't understand, and respect her perception.

YOU DON'T HAVE TO CATCH
EVERY BALL HE HITS TO YOU

W e often run off at the mouth just to talk. To fill the silences. You don't always have to respond, and if she's mumbling, which is the form these ramblings often take, you don't have to get irritated or constantly say, "What? I can't hear you." Not every comment is an invitation to converse.

YOU DON'T HAVE TO SWING AT EVERY STRIKE, EITHER

It's okay to pass over some remarks that you might disagree with. Pick and choose which ones are important enough to react to. If you know you are about to create ill feelings between you, and your differences are not that significant, learn to let it go. Put your energy into the big differences. In other words, don't sweat the little things.

WRITE A NOTE OR A LETTER IF CONVERSATION FAILS

Sometimes even the simplest of conversations between spouses get muddled and confused. Different conversational styles, points of view, levels of distraction—the reason doesn't matter. What's important is that you don't give up on expressing your ideas. Take the time to clarify your thoughts and write them down. Leave your letter or note in her pocket. When your partner reads it, she will have time to mull it over before responding.

SECRETS
CREATE
WALLS

WHEN HE TALKS ABOUT HIS DAYDREAMS, LET HIM

He says, "I want to spend a month alone on the top of a mountain." He may be in the midst of some kind of an emotional upheaval, or just talking. Let him talk. And let the moment pass—it's not about you. Address it only if the same conversation keeps repeating itself, in which case just ask, "Is this a daydream or a goal? It's beginning to concern me."

TAKE THE TIME TO BE CLEAR

Sometimes the words we use are clear to one of us but incomprehensible to the other. If you're not sure you understand what your partner is saying, ask her to say it another way. Don't just let it go. Ask again if you have to. Be certain you understand.

If you thought you got her point, but the conversation escalates into a fight, or subsequent remarks seem confusing, *ask*! Get clarification. What's the use of having a conversation if you don't understand one another?

DON'T HINT IF YOU CAN SAY IT...

"Is anybody cold here?" "Does anybody want to go to the movies?" "Do you think somebody needs to take out the garbage?"

Indirect communication, which seems innocent enough, can cause defensiveness and sometimes hostility. How can you tell when you're being indirect? Check out your heartbeat. Usually people don't say what's on their minds because they fear asserting themselves directly. Heart rates speed up, stomachs flutter, palms sometimes sweat. You'll feel a lot less stress if you can cut to the heart of what's bothering you, and say it. "I'm cold." "I'd like to go to the movies tonight." "Please take out the garbage." Be brave, say it honestly and directly. You'll cut through to real conversation that way.

...BUT IF YOU MUST HINT, FOLLOW THROUGH

You are understood by each other through how you express yourself, both verbally and non-verbally. A look—a smirk—a smile—a shrug—a sarcastic tone—a flinch—are signs of what you are thinking and feeling. In a marriage, these cues get to be known. Nothing is more crazy-making to your partner than your verbal denial of the emotions that are being trumpeted by your body language. Learn to be straightforward in matters of pain and joy.

COMMUNICATING

STOP DEFENDING YOURSELF AND HAVE A CONVERSATION

Look at the way you respond when your partner shows some kind of displeasure. If you feel you must defend yourself, that means you also think you are being attacked. Is this actually happening? Or is your partner simply asking for what she wants? Ask her if you're unsure of what she's saying. Don't create an unnecessary barricade between you, which is all that needless defense systems do.

AVOID QUESTIONS—LEARN TO MAKE STATEMENTS INSTEAD

Questions can be sincere efforts to obtain information, or destructively disguised hostile statements: "Why were you late?" "When are you going to get around to asking for that raise?" If you catch yourself using this means of communicating, try making a statement, beginning with the words "I feel" or "I wonder." If manipulative questions are a habit with you, try this: Have a conversation every day for a week without asking any questions. The payoff will be worth it.

TALK ABOUT YOUR FEELINGS
WITHOUT BLAMING AND
ACCUSING

When you have been hurt by something your partner has said or done, talk about it with the intent to furnish information, rather than to point your finger. "I was hurt when you forgot to introduce me to your boss, and I'd like you to try to remember to introduce me in the future." When you blame and accuse—"You forgot me again!"—you are making the assumption that your partner intended to make you feel that way. No one *makes* you feel anything.

PAY ATTENTION

Listening is an art anyone can learn. When you pay full attention, you create an atmosphere of trust and intimacy that will be rewarding to both of you. So don't channel surf when he's trying to talk to you. Show your attentiveness and regard by:

- Keeping eye contact
- Clarifying what you hear to make sure you've got it straight
- Acknowledging the value of his feelings

He'll love you for it!

PICK THE TIME AND PLACE CAREFULLY

When you want to engage your partner in a serious request or conversation, pick the time carefully. Contain yourself until it's appropriate to bring it up. Discussing upcoming tax payments in the middle of the playoffs usually doesn't work too well.

There will be times when you want to engage your partner in a serious request or conversation and you know it could be an inconvenient or inappropriate time. Say something like this to him: "There's something I want to discuss with you and I know this is a bad time. Let's put aside some time to do it later. I was thinking of — o'clock and maybe we can do it while we take a walk. Is that okay with you?" If he says no, then ask him to name the time. If it's an important enough conversation for you, negotiate for the time and place that you sense will be the most productive.

TALKING TO YOURSELF WON'T GET YOUR NEEDS MET

66 ead talk" can be useful if you are rehearsing for a job interview or a part in a play, but if you find yourself obsessing about what you shoulda-coulda-woulda said to your partner, it's destructive. You can't get heard by keeping the words in your head. Say them out loud to her. Tell her how you feel about what she has done or said, and ask her to discuss it with you. Continue the discussion until you both feel it is complete. Make sure you're done by asking, "Are we finished?"

COMMUNICATING

SHOWING
LOVE

LEW

"Please don't tell me you love me. Show me!"

When Gloria first said those words to me, I felt as if she were speaking in a foreign language. I saw myself as a pretty affectionate and attentive guy; I didn't understand what she wanted. (Of course, it didn't occur to me simply to ask her.)

Although Gloria didn't know it at the time, her "show me" request was often on my mind. One day I happened into a card shop. I had a flash of brilliance. Valentine's Day a month away, and the cards were on the rack.

I took a stab. I bought her a Valentine's Day card and sent it immediately. It was pretty mushy for the tough guy I thought I was, but I got a kick out of the wacky timing and thought the surprise might tickle Gloria.

"Tickle" turned out to be the understatement of the year. The response Gloria gave me when she received it was worthy of a conquering hero. I do remember saying something like, "Aren't you being a little excessive?" But she was sincere in her feelings, she insisted, since what I had done was the kind of thing she had asked for. Without realizing or planning it, I had stumbled on the key to Gloria's "show me." She loved the surprise, and even more, she loved seeing physical evidence that I had thought of her, and had paid attention to what she had said.

The payback for my little gesture was so far beyond the deed that I was encouraged to keep making similar gestures from time to time. The closeness these easy gifts created taught me a much-needed lesson early in our marriage. Affection and fun keep a marriage alive!

CATER TO HIS NEEDS WHEN HE'S STRESSED

Each of us has a different tolerance for stress, and at different times (of the day, week, month, year, or lifetime) we show it. If your partner snaps at you, before giving in to hurt or anger, look for the signs of stress. You will see it in your partner's facial expression or body language or irritable attitude. Or, maybe he will just even say "I'm all stressed out." This is not a time to argue. It's a time to give, to be more considerate than usual, to have empathy. It may be that all he needs is some time alone, or perhaps some extra touching. Be aware.

Try (gently):

- Offering a back or shoulder rub.
- Giving him time to himself if he wants it.
- Taking over some of his chores.
- Offering your help in solving the problem that created the stress.

SHOWING LOVE

BE ROMANTIC

Ah—romance. One of the important ways to keep the relationship alive. Find out what kinds of romantic desires your partner has—and make a gift of it. Any hour of the day or night is the right time for a romantic gesture to bring the two of you closer together.

You can do that by expressing your love as well as showing it. A birthday card when it's not her birthday says you're glad she was born. A single rose costs very little, but is very dear. The less expected, the greater the impact.

EXPECT NOTHING IN RETURN
AND YOU WON'T BE
DISAPPOINTED

D o what you do out of love. There is no rate of exchange.

SHOW LOVE THE WAY YOUR PARTNER SHOWS LOVE TO YOU

Take careful note of how she shows love to you. Notice the way she touches you and listens to you and the gifts she gives you. You will better understand how she wants love to be shown to her. Pay attention.

TAKE A LETTER, HONEY

Mail a love letter to your partner. With a stamp. Love letters shouldn't stop just because you live at the same address.

HOW NOT TO TAKE HER FOR GRANTED, IN PRIVATE

Nothing keeps a marriage alive like genuine, heartfelt . . . flattery! Be generous with compliments. *Notice* what you like about her—it will help keep your own fires burning. Write a list. Share it on your anniversary, or, better, read it to each other in bed once a week. (Guaranteed aphrodisiac, no extra charge.)

HOW NOT TO TAKE HIM FOR GRANTED, IN PUBLIC

D o what we just said on the preceding page at a party (not the aphrodisiac part, the flattery part). Tell anyone within your mate's hearing how great he looks. Or what an amazing job he did fixing the computer. Or changing the baby's diaper. Whatever. Make him complain you've embarrassed him. Have a fight about how much you love him and want the world to know. He'll love it.

LAVISH LOVE

Create a list of the many ways you can bestow love on your partner by doing for her what she would normally do for herself and for you. Spoil her.

BE PREPARED TO REASSURE
WHEN NEEDED

B e sensitive to your partner's insecurities. No matter how old he is, there are times when reassurance is needed to assuage fears. When you are tuned in to his feelings, you will know when to show your generosity and love. If you're not accustomed to the reassurer's role, start by just saying, "I'm here to help" and "I'm sorry you feel this way." He will feel better, knowing you're supportive and he does not have to suffer alone.

BE YOUR PARTNER'S CHEERLEADER

Very few people live in a world in which applause comes spontaneously. Partners in life can help to raise one another's self-esteem and enrich the quality of life by a cheerful and spontaneous show of admiration for efforts.

So what if you both feel silly? Give your partner a round of applause the next time she cooks you dinner. Shout hip hip hooray when he does the laundry—it goes a long way.

RULE 6

~

A SOLID MARRIAGE IS BASED ON MUTUAL RESPECT AND ADMIRATION

~

BECOME AN EXPERT ON EMPATHY

Learn to walk in your partner's shoes. In a loving relationship, you will be called upon to stop and listen and try to identify with your partner's feelings. Sometimes it's hard to do so because you feel the world so differently.

Practice. When your partner tells you a story, think hard and remember an experience that you had that was at least in some small part similar. After you remember the experience, try to remember the feeling as well. Once you've got it, say the words "I think I know how you feel. Is there anything I can do to help?" Or "I think I had a similar experience. This is what happened to me and how I felt. Is that what you're going through?"

SHOW UNCONDITIONAL LOVE

Unconditional love means that your partner is always assured of your love. There are going to be times when you don't approve of her actions. There will be times when she lets you down—big time. She may promise to call you when she's going to be late, then show up five hours late after you've called the hospitals. She may criticize you in public. No matter what she does, don't threaten to stop loving her. Tell her you hate what she did; tell her you're hurt; tell her you're furious. But don't ever imply you'll stop loving her. Your love is without conditions.

THINK ABOUT LOVING AS OFTEN AS POSSIBLE

Love fills empty spaces and otherwise difficult moments. If love is in your consciousness often, you will express it more often. Make her the star in your fantasies and tell her about it. The rewards are endless.

IT REALLY IS THE LITTLE THINGS

Everyone likes a surprise. We all like to feel special. A loving phone call, a playful gift, a love note when you're out of town, a special sexual surprise—whatever you do, it's a reminder that you're thinking about him.

GIVE YOUR PARTNER TIME ALONE WHEN YOU SENSE IT'S NEEDED

There are times when she may want to be alone and for some reason be reluctant to talk about it. If you sense that's what she wants, suggest it. Something special for her might be an afternoon, uninterrupted, to read a book, or go to a movie, or a night out with a friend. Whatever it is, honor it good-naturedly. What a gift!

CELEBRATE YOUR IN-BETWEEN ANNIVERSARIES

Do you remember the day you met? Your first kiss?

Over the years, a wedding anniversary can turn into an obligatory dinner out, not a true "celebration" of your commitment to one another. So try innovating—celebrate each other through recognizing events only the two of you know about. Make up new holidays for just the two of you and mark those special days on private calendars. Send a note, make a phone call, or go all out—just keep the obligation part light and the romance thick. Your secret celebrations will help you feel special, connected, and alive.

DO IT—DON'T JUST SAY IT

You show love by what you do in the relation-ship publicly as well as privately. Be mindful of what your partner needs to feel special. Put your arm around him. Make eye contact in a crowd. Touch his hair when he's driving. Hold hands.

PRAISE YOUR PARTNER
TO OTHERS

It's especially rewarding to your partner when he hears you have been saying good things about him to others. It reinforces your admiration for him and raises his self-esteem.

SHOW YOUR APPRECIATION

Say thanks. Say, "I appreciated it when you did that." There are few people who do more for us in our lifetime than our partners. Remember to say a simple "thank you." She'll thank you right back!

THINK ABOUT YOUR DEFINITION OF LOVE

Some believe that "if you love me . . . you will satisfy all of my needs and wishes." This definition of love burdens your partner with proving love at every turn. We like this definition: "Loving your partner is being as concerned for her/his well-being as you are for your own." Both of you write down your definitions. Exchange them. Talk about them.

CREATE MAGIC IN THE MARRIAGE

A magical marriage is punctuated by romance, mystery, and surprise. Giving some thought to new ways to provide those elements will reward you with a much more exciting and fun-filled relationship. Shock your partner by making a dinner reservation at a place he has casually mentioned. Buy tickets to a show you know he wants to see—or to a basketball game. Magic!

SAY GOOD NIGHT WITH LOVE

Here's one you've heard before—that's because it works. Some days do not end well. There may have been unresolved conflicts. Make a pact that one of the rules in your marriage is no matter what else is going on, neither of you will go to sleep angry, without expressing your feelings to your partner and giving you both a chance to resolve the bad feelings.

SEXUALITY

LEW

Sexual instinct is a common human trait, but sexuality is
a part of who we are as individuals as unique as each of
our personalities. In a marriage, two people with common
basic instincts, but entirely different wiring, are sexually involved. There are by definition going to be times when they
simply are not in sync.

When Gloria and I were newly married, we were intensely
attracted to one another's sexual energy. As we moved through
life, our sexuality was often influenced by whatever was happening in the rest of our lives. The pressures of health, work,
and family problems sometimes distracted us and reduced our
sexual energy.

As a young man, the responsibility I felt for the support of
our growing family sometimes lowered my sex drive. I turned
to male friends my own age for information and support. They
loudly denied they even knew what I was talking about and
were unable to admit they shared what I later learned was a
universal experience for almost all men at any stage of life.
(How difficult it was in those days to come to terms with our
humanness.)

I didn't know the key to healing the problem was right

there in bed beside me. I had no idea how to start the conversation. Finally, I just had to talk about it, and did, in some clumsy but sincere way. Gloria knew as little about it as I did in those days. But she did suggest that I talk to our family doctor. I did exactly that and learned from this kind and knowledgeable man that my fears were unnecessary and what was occasionally happening to me was experienced by all men at different times in their lives. That knowledge alone put my mind at ease and my body back on track.

Since then there continue to be occasional times in both our lives when we turn away from the intimacy that loving sexuality affords us. We become so involved in the management of our lives that we forget to enjoy the oasis from stress and the playfulness that our shared sexual feelings can provide. Now, when changes occur and there is the distance that lack of sexuality creates, we attempt to talk about it in a nonblaming or nonjudgmental manner. We have found it's vital to jump start our sexual feelings. We take time off from the business of life to become playmates. To rekindle our awareness of one another and complete our need for intimate contact.

RICHFIELDS'
RULE 7
～

NEVER
DISCLOSE
YOUR
PARTNER'S
CONFIDENCES
～

ADD TO YOUR SEXUAL EDUCATION

The more you know about sex and your partner, the more fun your sex life is going to be. Be open to the rainbow of methods for mutual pleasure.

Read one of the many books available on the subject, or, if you're so inclined, investigate sexual catalogs and videos. Bookstores have entire sections devoted to sexuality. If these methods seem a bit impersonal, try reading a romantic novel to one another, and then talking about what you've read (and expanding on what's between the lines).

ENJOY THE AFTERGLOW

There really is an afterglow. It's a time for pillow talk, holding one another, and finishing your sexual time with tenderness and love.

KEEP YOUR SEX LIFE CONFIDENTIAL

Talking to anyone else about your sexual relationship is a breach of confidentiality. What you discuss with your partner, or when, how, and how often you have sex, must always be kept solely between the two of you. This is the foundation of a trusting sexual relationship.

A NEAT RETREAT

Leaving cosmetics all over the bathroom counter, dropping socks and clothing on the floor, can throw a wet blanket on sexual desire. Each of you, take care to keep the bedroom a special, personal, and inviting place.

TAKE RESPONSIBILITY FOR YOUR OWN SEXUALITY

Your partner may sometimes feel overburdened with the responsibility of satisfying your sexual needs if they are different from hers. It's your job to get to know your own body, so that you can help your partner help you to get the greatest gratification from the sex act. If you don't know your body, you can't take the lead and share what your needs are—and both of you will be the worse off for it. Know yourself—and teach each other.

SEX TALK

A talk about sexual needs and feelings can be among the most difficult conversations, even between couples who feel very close to one another. We're brought up to consider sexual feelings taboo, certainly not something for open conversation. If you find talking about sex difficult, you might find these ideas helpful in lessening your fear and inhibitions:

• Start talking about sex by talking indirectly. Don't feel you must jump right into revealing your hidden passions. Instead, read a book or an article together and talk about it.

• Personally identify with what you're reading and, as you're comfortable, start to talk about your feelings with your partner.

• Never accuse your partner of being inadequate. If she's not doing something you need, say "I'd like you to" rather than "you never do."

ALLOW TIME AFTER AN ARGUMENT TO RECONNECT SEXUALLY

Different people need different amounts of time to recover from an argument. After you argue, respect your partner's need for distance (even if you feel quite the opposite). If she balks when you approach her, be sensitive to her cues and don't take offense. Your respectful treatment will cement the trust between you and hasten the resolution of the argument and all its effects.

RULE 8

NOTHING TURNS
A WOMAN ON
SO MUCH
AS BEING
UNQUESTIONABLY
SEEN AND HEARD

ENRICH YOUR SEX LIFE WITH PERPETUAL TRUST

Trust is a significant part of a fully alive marriage. A special sexual relationship is dependent upon each of you knowing you will be secure both physically and emotionally. Make trust a priority by being considerate of each other's vulnerabilities. Be trustworthy—in bed and out.

SAY GOOD-BYE TO SEXUAL GUILT

Some of the messages you no doubt got when you were a child, either overtly or covertly, were incorporated into your adult life. You carry those messages with you into bed.

Take a close look at your sexual self. Can you find attitudes and beliefs that don't really fit your adult desires? The following exploration may help:

- Make a list of everything you've learned about sexual rights and wrongs.
- Check which ones you believe today.
- Ask yourself which of these beliefs are interfering with your sexual pleasure; indicate them with an "X."
- Ask yourself what you are willing to try changing; ask your partner if he has the same desires.
- Introduce one change at a time, giving yourselves enough time between changes to integrate your new feelings.

EXPECT SOME SEXUAL EXPERIENCES TO BE MORE GRATIFYING THAN OTHERS

Each time you are together sexually, you will experience varying levels of passion. There may not be a completion each time, or one of you will feel more in the mood than the other. Keep in mind that there's always tomorrow—and the day after.

INCLUDE SPONTANEITY IN
YOUR LOVE LIFE

There's a time for prolonged sensuality, which creates greater intimacy between you. And there is a time for a quick and sudden burst of passion, which can be fun. Allow the full range of possibilities.

CHANGE YOUR SEXUAL ROUTINE

Creating change in how, when, and where you have sex keeps the spice in your marriage and a smile on your face. A sexual encounter with your partner that is not predictable can be rejuvenating. So much of our lives are planned and lived according to a schedule—a time for this and a time for that.

While there's certainly nothing wrong with planning a regular night for, and style of, sexual intimacy, don't hesitate to try something new now and then, and be open if your partner has taken the initiative to introduce change. (By the same token, if your partner is not in the mood for your innovations, back off and try again another day.)

RULE 9

NOTHING TURNS
A MAN ON
SO MUCH AS
HIS PARTNER
MAKING HIM FEEL
ATTRACTIVE
AND DESIRED

THERE'S MORE TO SEX THAN INTERCOURSE

You can show your desire and appreciation for one another in many ways. Feeling sexual is another way to feel good about yourself and your partner. These feelings can be generated by an intense intimate conversation that allows for vulnerability, having fun together, enjoying sensuality without setting goals for intercourse. Sexual feelings do not always have to end in orgasm. Merely being close and validating your love can create satisfying sensuality.

ALLOW YOURSELF YOUR TRUE SEXUAL FEELINGS

There are going to be periods in your life when your sex drive is at a low ebb. Work problems, illness, and attention to child care are a few of the reasons this can happen—and does happen, to everyone. During these times:

- *Talk about it*. Let your partner in on how you feel. Tell him you still love and desire him. Assure him sex is just "on hold" temporarily.
- Show affection by holding and touching your partner.
- Make a date for sex and keep it. Literally. Book a room in a hotel, go on vacation—create a specific plan for jump starting your sexual feelings.

ENJOY YOUR SEXUAL FANTASIES

Fantasies are just fantasies. Sharing fantasies in your sex life should enrich and enhance it, not inhibit it. Shared fantasies can create greater intimacy; do be sensitive about which fantasies you choose to share with your partner, though. Share fantasies that you believe will turn you both on, or those that help you articulate an inoffensive sexual need. Have fun together with your fantasies!

MAKING LOVE LAST
ALL DAY LONG

Foreplay can begin in the morning when you kiss one another good-bye. Follow it up with a phone call during the day when you tell her you're thinking about her. A little hint or tease hours in advance of being together can create excitement in the anticipation. Desire is built over time. The more time you give it, the higher the level of excitement.

PAY ATTENTION TO YOUR PARTNER'S UNIQUE SEXUAL NEEDS

For many men, women's bodies are a complete mystery. (You know the joke: It's not called the G-spot; it's called the W-spot. She asks me to find it and I say W-w-w-what?) Each of us is wired in a special way; therefore it's necessary to take note of her verbal and nonverbal responses during your lovemaking. Your partner has her own special ways of telling you what she desires, even if she isn't saying the words. Pay attention. Pay attention. Pay attention.

Be aware of your partner's breathing, of her body's responses. Learn her body through nonsexual massage. If you don't know if something is working, ask. And, pay attention.

DIFFERENCES

GLORIA

We had recently moved into a new community and were attending a home owners' meeting. Arriving late, we found single seats across the room from one another. The topic of the meeting was whether to hire security guards for the community.

Lew jumped up and said he believed that the guards were not necessary given their exorbitant cost. I had never (openly) disagreed with Lew before—this was in the mid-fifties, and our marriage was quite traditional—but here I felt I had to speak out. No one there knew we were married. Before I knew it, I was standing and debating. I thought a guard would give us a greater sense of safety and the added expense would be worth it, and I said so. Strenuously. The debate became lively and emphatic.

After the meeting closed, we walked arm in arm back to our car. Our new neighbors watched. It was dawning on them that we were married, and they clearly were amazed. Wives didn't disagree with their husbands in public in those days.

Lew and I didn't care. We felt wonderful and aglow in a way. There was something exciting about the event. It was like courting all over, getting to see each other as entirely separate.

That experience, and many others like it as time has passed, has taught us to encourage and enjoy the freedom to express our differences. It helps keep our marriage passionate—and fully alive.

Rule 10

&

LASTING
LOVE
IS BUILT
ON RESPECT
FOR
DIFFERENCES

&

THE WAYS YOU ARE DIFFERENT

You are different, separate people coming together in marriage. You will find you have different opinions on many subjects, different reactions, different world views. Some of the issues that divide you may be:

Money (what to spend it on and how to invest and save it)

Sex (frequency, quality, and sensitivity)

People (whom you like or dislike to spend time with)

Food (how much—where—with whom—what kind)

Politics (opinions)

Sports (watching, playing, time spent, choices)

Public behavior (extrovert, introvert)

Time (early, late)

Vacations (where, when, how much time to spend)

Expressions of feelings (too much, not enough)

As distinct as these issues are, the resolution of disagreements over each follows a similar pattern. We think of this as our own personal *peace* plan—and we happily share it with you:

PEACE

P - Placate: Calm yourself so that you can have a discussion in a mature fashion.

E - Evaluate: Decide its relative importance. On a scale of one to ten, how important is it, really?

A - Accept: Consent to allow your partner to be different. Loving someone includes accepting him as he is.

C - Compromise: Find the harmony in your differences. A one-note song can be very boring.

E - Enjoy: Find pleasure for yourself in your separate self; identifying the positive aspects of your dissimilarities could create fun and excitement for both of you.

P = PLACATE
YOUR WAY IS NOT MY WAY

He's a creature of habit, you like to wing it. Each of you finds comfort in your particular mode of living. Your approach to routine brings you comfort, and you can guess that he finds comfort in his approach. You may or may not have known about your differences when you got married. Calm yourself and put your criticism on hold. Look inward, not out. Your dissimilarities are not a reason for dispute.

E = EVALUATE
APPRECIATE YOUR
DISSIMILARITY

Being different offers you the opportunity to learn from one another. One of you may be lively and gregarious, the other serious. Your personality differences are probably what attracted you to each other in the first place. The balance between you is a tremendous advantage in fulfilling your greatest potential as a couple. Together, you provide the missing parts in one another.

A = ACCEPT
WHY IS IT THAT MY REASONABLE MIND DOESN'T CONNECT WITH YOUR REASONABLE MIND?

You bring to each other different ways of looking at things. You are each made up of your genes, your cultural backgrounds, your age, and your life experiences. It's rare when two people have a perfect fit from the beginning. But, if you're in the marriage for the long haul, take the time to know yourself, to know your partner, and to reveal yourselves to each other to the best of your abilities. Confirming each other will create the opportunity for greater empathy and closeness, and a fully alive marriage.

C = COMPROMISE
LOVING EACH OTHER IS
ONE THING,
LIVING TOGETHER IS
QUITE ANOTHER

You like the windows open. He likes them closed. You like lots of blankets. He likes few. You like parties. He likes small groups. Etc. Etc. Now, what do you do?

First, identify these things as differences. Do not criticize or ridicule your partner. See a difference as a temporary disharmony, and an opportunity to learn the art of compromise and negotiation. Remember, you are together because you love one another, not because you were perfectly matched.

DIFFERENCES

E = ENJOY
TAKE PLEASURE IN YOUR DIFFERENCES

Look in the mirror. You are a unique person. You each came into this marriage with different histories, attitudes, and habits. Rather than feeling one-down or struggling for the upper hand when she is expressing herself, tune in and enjoy her all the more.

CONFLICT

LEW AND GLORIA

*S*ome of the worst times we've spent together in our forty-six-year marriage have been on our anniversaries. The anniversary dinners would start out very well with happy anticipation as we hunted for unusual and romantic new restaurants. The tension started, time after time, after we toasted the number of years together and one or the other of us would begin to talk about what was missing in our marriage. We forced ourselves to keep our voices down so we wouldn't drown out the other guests. The muscles in our jaws and necks were so tense by the end of these evenings, it felt like it would take forever to unlock them. As for romance—forget it!

This happened just about every anniversary for a number of years. It seemed the more we focused on "just us" away from life's distractions, the more likely we were to find problems. Did this mean, we wondered, that between anniversaries we were hiding our feelings behind jobs and kids and that we really didn't know each other? We feared that the conflict at hand was a sign of something deeper, that we were not only fighting today's fight, but all of yesterday's fights, and perhaps foreshadowing worse fights for tomorrow.

We eventually learned through our studies and our prac-

CONFLICT

tices that our "anniversary dances" were common and understandable events. Because our lives were busy, and anniversaries truly were a rare opportunity to focus on the marriage, it was natural that both good and bad feelings we hadn't taken the time to express were going to come up. These fights didn't mean our marriage was a fake during the rest of the year, but they did signal that we'd benefit from learning to communicate without going ballistic (realizing the fights were predictable helped) and that we probably needed to take a little more time to focus on our marriage on those not-so-special occasions.

Our old anniversary battles have now become a family joke. Of course, we still face occasional conflicts—sometimes, yes, on our anniversaries. While we now recognize that not every difference has to turn into a conflict, and that allowances must be made for disagreements in a close relationship, we also believe that a truly alive marriage is one in which two different people feel free to openly and directly express their opinions. In such a marriage conflict is inevitable and when dealt with boldly and resolved honestly, it will keep the marriage vital.

Rule 11

❧

COMPROMISE IS AN ESSENTIAL PART OF A HAPPY MARRIAGE

❧

FIGHT WITHOUT FLIGHT

Human beings react to stress in a very predictable fashion—it makes them want to fight or run. The stress of a dispute in your marriage makes you want to say things such as "Let's just get a divorce," or "I don't know how long I can put up with this," or "You don't love me anymore." Banish those words from your disputes. They're counterproductive and come from nothing but fear. Work it out without the threats—it will be much more effective.

LET GO OF RESENTMENTS AND
MAKE ROOM FOR LOVE

Get those old resentments out of your mind. Here's how: Write down all those nagging memories of arguments past. Keep writing until you've written everything you can think of. Take a few days or a few weeks to do this. Keep your writing to yourself. Read it over when you decide you have written everything there is to say. When you're ready, put the paper aside. Take out another piece of paper, just as long, and write, for each resentment: "It's in the past and over. I will live with it." In a personal and private ritual (or, if you feel it's appropriate, with your mate), burn both papers and let your resentments go up in smoke.

RESPECT YOUR PARTNER'S LOW TOLERANCE FOR CONFLICT

Keeping eye contact and staying in a conflict for a protracted period of time is hard to do for some people. Some feel anxious and want to run away. It's important to understand your partner's tolerance for direct confrontation and to respect his needs. If your partner has a low tolerance for conflict and you need to discuss something at length, use a timer. Really! Set it for one minute and maintain eye contact while you talk about a problem. Stop and take time-out when the timer goes off. Set the timer again, this time for two minutes, continue the discussion, then take time-out. Keep adding minutes until you have reached the end of the discussion (or the end of your partner's patience). It may seem ridiculous in the beginning, but this method works and can help resolve those arguments that keep popping up again and again because they are left unfinished.

LEAVE OTHERS' OPINIONS OUT
OF THE DISCUSSION

Sometimes you may want to strengthen your point of view by telling your partner that other people think and say the same thing you are saying. This is a real no-no! Don't bring in the troops! It can cause even more problems in the future when your partner either turns her back on that person or confronts the person with what you told her. Remember that this discussion is between *just the two of you*. If she wants to know what other people think, she'll ask you!

KNOW WHAT THE DISPUTE
IS ABOUT

Arguments often escalate into world wars, taking twists and turns and lasting forever because we tend to expand each present disagreement to encompass all past wounds. A simple way to avoid this is to force yourselves to keep a narrow focus on the conflict at hand. When the argument starts, pause. Even in your anger, spell out the parameters of your disagreement and agree on the specific issue you'll be discussing—then keep the fight in the ring.

RICHFIELDS'
RULE 12

FIGHTING HURTS— DISCUSSION HEALS

STAY ON THE TRACK UNTIL THE FINISH LINE

Once the disagreement begins, stick to the subject until you have both agreed that you are satisfied with the result. If you haven't finished the discussion, and seem to be getting tired or frustrated, set a specific time to finish (the sooner, the better) so you can get back to life's pleasures.

RESOLVE CONFLICTS SO YOU BOTH WIN

If you have a fight and you win, you may realize that you both lose after all—if the loser withdraws, seeks revenge, pouts, storms out, or gets depressed. The best resolutions leave something on the table for both partners to feel good about. That way you both come through as winners.

Listen to your partner even when you disagree. She may have something to say that is of value. Pay attention, also, to how badly you need to be a victor. Don't let your ego's need to be completely right leave you victorious but lonely.

TAKE RESPONSIBILITY FOR
YOUR MISTAKES

If your partner feels hurt by what you said or did, even if (especially if) you had no intention of hurting her, don't defend yourself! In the beginning of the discussion say, simply, "I'm sorry I hurt you." Crying "I didn't do it" is more hurtful to your partner than whatever you have said or done. Remember that you're human and are expected to err from time to time.

In order for the experience to feel complete, you both will need to express your viewpoints, but the hurt has to begin to heal first.

WHEN TEMPERATURES RISE

Just when the argument gets really hot, try this. (You'll feel silly. Try it anyway.) Call a time-out. Take a deep breath and say (shout if you have to), together if you can, "We will work this out!"

Why do this? The impact of a stated and shared positive outlook can be astounding. Simply acknowledging you believe in the future will defuse the hostility and help you resolve the real issues. If you tell one another that you can work it out, you will.

NEGATIVE EXPERIENCES ARE A GUARANTEED PART OF MARRIAGE

There will be times when you're not happy in your marriage, when being around your partner makes you uncomfortable, not comforted. Often, what causes this type of distance is a buildup of unfinished business between you. You really have no choice here. You must tell your partner you're not happy and try to explain why. And you must do it right away. Without anger, without blame, state it as a problem for both of you that you want to solve.

Sometimes, an overwhelming negative feeling cannot be worked out between you, and an outsider can help. Many times, though, you will be amazed at how quickly a two-ton cloud can lift when you simply face it honestly. It takes courage, but take heart. If you are willing to face the issue between you head-on, both of you will come out winners.

RICHFIELDS'
Rule 13

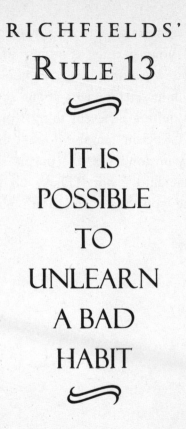

IT IS
POSSIBLE
TO
UNLEARN
A BAD
HABIT

CRITICS BELONG AT THE MOVIES

Of course throughout your marriage (maybe daily!) your partner is going to say or do something that you don't like, and you're going to tell him. An honest statement about something on your mind is quite a different thing from deliberate faultfinding. Criticism simply doesn't belong in a marriage. If you don't like the purple shirt, say "I don't like that shirt," not "That's an ugly shirt." Don't analyze your mate and don't pick on him. Period.

... AND JUDGES BELONG IN COURT

Judges belong in a court of law. You may have your own ideas about many things: how a person should behave, what should be said, how one should appear. Ideas and opinions are one thing, setting your opinions up as unimpeachable truth is quite another. You don't like that purple shirt? If you say (to yourself or to him) "People who buy shirts like that have no taste," look out—you're about to fall off your bench, Your Honor.

Being judgmental is a learned technique and it can be unlearned. It takes a good look in a mirror, though. A quick catch of your own thoughts. Have you proven your partner guilty without a trial? That's not fair in any court, and has no place in a marriage.

SOLVE THE PROBLEMS BETWEEN
YOU AS QUICKLY AS POSSIBLE

Don't sit on your anger. Don't be too proud to be the first one to say you're hurt. Don't wait to confront and don't wait to apologize. As soon as you have her attention, get the matter out and done with.

GET A MEDIATOR IF YOU CAN'T RESOLVE IT YOURSELVES

You've tried, and you can't find a way to get comfortable with one another about a particular subject. And the bad feelings are getting in the way of your being together in a loving way. It's time to find a mediator—in the form of a counselor, therapist, pastor, or rabbi. Don't wait forever—when you know you've tried all you know how, make that phone call!

GROWTH

LEW

Your partner's need to change and grow is an individual force having nothing whatsoever to do with your marriage. Your partner's growth may upset you. You may feel as though you're being left behind. You may feel there is something wrong with you if you don't have the same energy directed toward change and growth as she does.

Your partner's desire for personal change can sometimes be frightening. The fear comes in part from the fact that change is often accompanied by a sense of loss of the familiar and comfortable.

Many years ago I was a sales executive and had to spend a great deal of time away from home. During this period, Gloria decided she wanted to work. The children were independent, in school all day, and she had the time.

She went to work at the office of the local school district. A whole new world of interesting people who were intensely involved in the community and education appeared in her life.

Her new world consumed her. I felt upset and uncomfortable about this for months before I even realized why. I really felt very insecure—I had never been to college and all these people had. I was a salesman, wearing my three-piece suit and pocket protector, drinking gin when they drank wine. I walked into my own house to find all these strangers wearing flowered shirts and beads and talking books. I started attacking Gloria through innuendo. I criticized her new friends—people I hardly knew. I told her her job sounded boring to me. The number of little squabbles interrupting our marriage—about which movie we should see, or household chores, multiplied.

Somehow, Gloria had learned enough by that time to ask me: "What is really going on here, Lew?" Gloria probed and probed; I denied and denied. But she stayed with it until my defenses came down, and in a moment I blurted out what seemed to me at the time to be a weak and even unmanly admission. I was very afraid that things might change between us, and I was afraid of being left behind.

Gloria took control. She made a point of including me in her circle of new friends who somehow suddenly became much less threatening after I let myself get to know them. The feeling of being an outsider left me.

We both realized that talking about the changes I perceived were taking place had calmed me down. Our support for one another grew, blossoming into greater intimacy and creativity.

EXPLORE YOURSELF

Socrates said it best: "A life which is unexamined is not worth living." It's become almost cliché now; nonetheless, the happiness self-knowledge can bring to a marriage is limitless. There are many paths available to you today. You can learn to be a witness to your own thoughts and actions through books, retreats, conversations, or therapy. As you discover yourself, you will learn to separate childhood longings from adult emotions, to rely less on your partner to fill unexpressed needs and more on yourself as a contributor to an equal and fulfilling relationship.

KEEP YOUR RELATIONSHIP OUT OF THE BLENDER

It's very easy for us to get the influential people in our lives all mixed up. Take a good look at your partner. She is not your old girlfriend who may have hurt or disappointed you. She is not your mother.

It can be hard to catch yourself doing this. Here are some cues: Does your anger, upon reflection, seem out of proportion to the event? Does your partner say to you on occasion, "What are you talking about? I don't do that. That's not me."

Once it occurs to you that you're answering your mother when your mate asks you to take out the garbage, stop before you speak. Tell yourself, "This is not my mother. This is my partner and I *don't need* to rebel."

SUPPORT HER EFFORTS TO CHANGE A BAD HABIT

Stopping smoking or drinking, stopping nail biting, changing diet—these are hard to do. She
needs all the support and encouragement she can get,
but she doesn't need a second conscience. "Support"
means asking her if and how you can help and then
doing it; it means noticing when she's doing well and
complimenting her briefly (no gushing). "Support"
doesn't mean watching her every move, or pressuring
her, or berating her when she fails, or, above all, ex-
pecting instant results. Changing habits can take
time—and sometimes doesn't work at all. The effort
itself is worth your respect.

YOU'RE NOT PERFECT . . .

Guess what? You're not perfect. You make mistakes. You use bad judgment; you have bad hair days and poppy seeds in your teeth. You can be wrong and admit it in an argument and your partner will hold you in just as much esteem—probably more. Try this—see what happens next time you know you've made a mistake and you say, "Sorry, I made a mistake." Does the world end? Laughing at yourself is a lot more fun than holding yourself to a standard only a saint could attain. Give yourself a break!

... AND NEITHER IS SHE

And while you're at it, give your partner a break, too. At times your partner will be either self-centered, impolite, out of sorts, or something that you can't believe she could be. So be it. You don't have to comment on every mistake, and for heaven's sake don't let a negative trait cause you to rethink the whole relationship. Pedestals are for statues—let her jump off hers with glee and love her more for her humanness.

THE ENCHANTED COTTAGE

An old movie we love told the story of two people in love, both of whom were horribly burned, but saw each other in their youthful beauty when they retreated to their "enchanted cottage." When your partner's changes throw you off balance, use this as a metaphor—we do. We all age: hair thins and grays, bellies grow—even opinions can shift. Think of your marriage as an enchanted cottage. See your partner in all his essential wonder, regardless of the inevitable changes.

RULE 14

TOUCHING
EACH OTHER'S
INNER WORLD
IS THE
ESSENCE OF
INTIMACY

EMBRACE CHANGE

When you hear yourself saying: "I can't help it—it's just who I am!" listen carefully. You *can* help it, you know. You weren't born this way. These words show an unwillingness to even attempt to change. Rigidity and inflexibility don't fit well in an ever-evolving, loving marriage. Simply because you've always done it your way doesn't mean you can't try to make an adjustment in your habit or attitude. So: banish "That's just me!" from your vocabulary. Now and always.

SUPPORT YOUR PARTNER'S SEARCH FOR SELF-DISCOVERY

You have everything to gain by encouraging your partner to get to know himself better, through whatever means he chooses. In the beginning of your partner's self-exploration he'll probably be pretty tough to live with. Stick with him and wait it out. When he learns to look at himself through a clearer lens, you'll find you have a more interesting partner, more authentic conversations, and a more intimate, vibrant relationship.

BE WHO YOU ARE

The stronger you are in your own sense of identity, the easier it will be for your marriage to weather the many exterior changes that happen to each of you individually. If, for example, your "self" is defined by your work, and you lose your job, you lose your self. Without this sense of self, you can become overly dependent on your partner for your sense of identity.

This is not an easy issue for most of us. Rely on the strength of your marriage to help. Set aside one evening. Together, write self-descriptions and partner-descriptions. Use the headings *How I see me* and *How I see you*. List, for yourself and your partner, personality traits, your likes, what you do well, what you dislike, what you'd like to learn, and whatever else comes to your mind. Exchange your lists. Have fun talking about them, emphasizing to each other those qualities you think are especially definitive and wonderful.

TAKE A DEEP BREATH AND
COUNT TO TEN

Do you react to life's everyday events as though they were life or death experiences? Geniuses have been saying this for generations—and they're right. Relax! Learn to put the moment into perspective when you get uptight. Ask yourself how important the problem is. Chill out and let the moment pass.

SUPPORT YOUR LOCAL FANTASY

Encourage your partner to recognize and share with you his dreams and visions. Share your own with him. No judgments allowed. This is the pathway to intimacy. Play "what if" together. Ask each other "What if we had a million dollars, what would we do? What would you do? What would I do?" Dream separately and together.

FIND TIME TO GET AWAY—ALONE

Getting away by yourself, even for a few hours, gives you an opportunity to get acquainted with yourself again. This can be done through meditation, a bike ride, or anything that gratifies you. The result is often increased desire to be with your partner.

WALK WITH THE SLOWEST WALKER

People change and grow at different rates of speed. When learning a sport, studying a new language, or figuring out the VCR, one of you will learn faster than the other. The same applies when it comes to maturing psychologically or socially. In order to maintain closeness and enjoyment in your marriage, it is important to accommodate each other and pace yourself accordingly. Patience, empathy, acceptance are the passwords to remember so that you can walk side by side.

RICHFIELDS'
Rule 15

~

COUNT
ON THE
FACT THAT
LIFE DOESN'T
ALWAYS GO
ACCORDING
TO PLAN

~

SUPPORT YOUR PARTNER'S DESIRE FOR INDIVIDUAL ACTIVITIES

When your partner wants to experience activities alone or with another group, you might be worried and think things like: "Does this mean you don't like me? Or love me? Or that you're showing signs of leaving me?" Doing things separately means nothing of the kind. Each of you must honor your individuality, occasionally exploring interests on your own. The newly knowledgeable self your partner brings back to the marriage can enhance your life together and add energy to your relationship. Enjoy your now-more-interesting partner—and let her know it!

THINK BEFORE YOU ACT

Apologies are important. But are you apologizing again and again for the same behavior? It's time to take notice and make an effort to change. Even a sincere "I'm sorry" gets old after a while—if you are really sorry, make your best effort to avoid the behavior in the future. Both you and your partner will appreciate it.

GROW ALONG WITH ME

It's as important to grow together as it is to grow separately. Together, walk a new path. Drive a different road. Try another kind of meal. Visit an out-of-the-ordinary place. Learn a new language. When you do these things together, you bring new light and pleasure to your marriage. It's never too late to introduce a new experience into your relationship. Be imaginative—have fun—life is short!

TAKE IN COMPLIMENTS

Don't ever throw away a compliment. Even when it's hard, believe it! (You may have to start by acting as if you believe it—so act.) Maybe you were brought up to be humble, not to "show off" or "blow your own horn." But accepting praise when it comes your way is a way of filling your bank account of self-esteem. Say, "Thank you." He will be pleased that you value his opinion.

LEAVE YOUR DAILY BAGGAGE
AT THE GYM

When you know you've had an upsetting day, even if you think it's over, think again. Make sure to take whatever time you need to separate the unpleasantness of your workday from your home. Let your partner in on how you feel. As soon as you can, tell your partner you need time to blow off steam and find a nonthreatening way to do it.

RULE 16

~

EVERYONE
HAS THE
POWER
TO
CHANGE

~

LEARN YOUR PARTNER'S HOPES AND DREAMS

Each individual has different aspirations and yearnings. Take the opportunity to learn about your partner's dreams and make the effort to help him attain them. Talk to him about those dreams. Ask him pointed or provocative questions. Respect his most far-reaching ideals.

FORGIVE

In your marriage, as the years go by, you may hurt one another deeply. You won't intend to, but it will happen. After it happens, long after it's over and done with, you will still occasionally remember the experience and possibly relive the pain.

History can't be changed. It can only serve us by the lessons it teaches. Holding on to unpleasant memories keeps you from living fully in the present and prevents you from moving on. So talk to your partner about the memories that disturb you. But if your partner cannot help to shift your uncomfortable feelings, talk to a friend or write about the unfinished business in your journal. And, if all of the above fails, make an appointment to talk to a therapist. It's your job to forgive and move on. The future is worth it.

STAY MARRIED

There are times when the marriage goes stale, or becomes uncomfortable. Don't give up. A marriage that once worked can work again. There is a big payoff.

Human beings need to connect, and to connect deeply. There are good reasons to stay married; hanging in there during the difficult times brings you, if you do the work, to a deeper level of intimacy that feels wonderful. There's little as rewarding in life as the knowledge that there's someone with whom you share history, familiarity, and the emotional rewards of joining in one goal—your marriage and each other's happiness in that marriage.

Life is hard. It's easier together.

TOGETHER
FOREVER

W e ask ourselves why we struggled so mightily to stay together through the difficult periods of our marriage, when all around us couples were bitterly separating. As we look back, we can see that the attraction we originally felt for each other remained alive, though partially buried under an ever-increasing mound of bad communication, unrealistic expectations, fights for control, and selfish demands.

During the early times, we made what we believe to be an important discovery. We learned that each time we successfully negotiated with each other to work through our problems, we ultimately felt closer and happier. As time passed, with each problem we conquered together, our confidence grew—and we felt stronger and stronger in our marriage, having managed to navigate yet another very bumpy road. We started to believe that together we would be able to surmount new obstacles as they inevitably leaped in our way.

With each resolved conflict, we learned to stop asking each other to fulfill our own individual neurotic demands. As the layers of discontent were bulldozed away, we recognized that our emotional tie to one another was too rare and strong to walk away from. We began to trust each other, noticing that neither one of us had given up. We each began to feel safe in counting on the other to continue to make the choice to find *ways to blend the individual need for freedom and personal expression with the communal needs of our marriage.*

Growing old together may seem like a cliché to young couples. For many, it may simply be a dream or a scene from an old Jimmy Stewart movie. As we look through our bifocals at each other and at our history, we can see that the effort we put into our marriage throughout the years paid off in pure joy. We have negotiated the rapids, climbed to the highest peaks, and we did it together.

TOGETHER FOREVER!